Mrs Gaskell's

The Well at Pen-Morfa

Peter Leigh

Published in association with The Basic Skills Agency

Hodder & Stoughton

A MEMBER OF THE HODDER HEADLINE GROUP

Acknowledgements
Cover: Matthew Williams
Illustrations: Jim Eldridge
Photograph of Mrs Gaskell © The Hulton Getty Picture Collection Limited

Orders: please contact Bookpoint Ltd, 39 Milton Park, Abingdon, Oxon OX14 4TD. Telephone: (44) 01235 400414, Fax: (44) 01235 400454. Lines are open from 9.00–6.00, Monday to Saturday, with a 24 hour message answering service. Email address: orders@bookpoint.co.uk

British Library Cataloguing in Publication Data
A catalogue record for this title is available from The British Library

ISBN 0 340 74311 5

First published 1999
Impression number   10 9 8 7 6 5 4 3 2 1
Year   2005 2004 2003 2002 2001 2000 1999

Copyright © 1999 Peter Leigh

Typeset by Fakenham Photosetting Ltd, Fakenham, Norfolk.
Printed in Great Britain for Hodder & Stoughton Educational, a division of Hodder Headline Plc, 338 Euston Road, London NW1 3BH by Redwood Books, Trowbridge, Wiltshire.

About the author

Mrs Gaskell was born in 1810 and died in
1865.
She wrote about ordinary people,
especially women,
and the hardship of their lives.

About the story

This story is set in Wales

The people in it are Eleanor and Nest,
who are mother and daughter,
Edward Williams,
who wants to marry Nest,
and Mary Williams (no relation
to Edward),
a half-crazy woman
who comes to live with Nest.

I

At Pen-Morfa in Wales
there is a beautiful well.
It lies at the foot of a cliff.

There are some large sloping stones
that lead to the well,
which are covered in bright moss
and golden lichen.

lichen – a fungus
that grows on rocks

Nearby is a village.
Many years ago, there lived in the village
a widow called Eleanor Gwynn
and her daughter Nest.
Eleanor was neither rich nor poor,
but to all the young men she was very rich,
because her daughter was lovely,
more beautiful than anyone for miles around.

She tried to please all,
both old and young, men and women.
For everyone she had a sweet smile,
a word of kindness, and a merry glance.
But some took her smiles and kind words
wrongly,
and called her a flirt.
Her mother heard it and sighed,
but Nest only laughed.

It was her job to fetch water from the well.
People say it was the prettiest sight
to see her stepping lightly over the stones.
The pail of water balanced on her head –
she didn't need to steady it with her hand.
They also say there was no better daughter
to a widowed mother, than Nest Gwynn.

Near the village lived a young farmer
called Edward Williams.
People said he was looking for a wife.
They told Nest so,
but she tossed her head and reddened,
and said he might look for a long time
before he got one.

Nest is saying
she's not interested
in him. Do you think
she means this?

2

So it was no surprise
that one morning when she went to the well,
Edward Williams happened to be there.
Somehow her pail of water was spilt,
and it seemed to take her a very long time
to fill it again!

Why, do you think?

When she came home
she threw her arms round her mother's neck,
and cried with happiness.
She told her that Edward Williams
had asked her to marry him,
and that she had said 'Yes.'

Eleanor cried too, but later and alone.
She was happy for Nest,
but would miss her in a thousand ways.

But she couldn't be sad for long,
while Nest was so happy.

Nest danced and sang more than ever,
and then sat silent, and smiled to herself.

If you spoke to her, she started,
and came back to the present
with a scarlet blush,
which showed what she had been thinking of.
That was a sunny, happy time.
But it was not to last.

One fine frosty morning
Nest went out with Edward.
She was wearing her best cloak and new hat.
She seemed specially lovely.

Edward had some work to attend to,
and left her in the village.
She went on to the well.

The water over the slanting stones had
frozen,
and was a coat of ice.

Poor Nest fell,
and put out her hip.
She screamed once or twice in pain,
and then fainted.

ice-glued – the water has frozen, and stuck Nest to the rock

A child, coming past an hour later,
saw her lying there,
ice-glued to the stone,
and thought she was dead.

'Nest Gwynn is dead! Nest Gwynn is dead!'
she cried as she ran through the village.

Everyone came out in alarm,
and went running to the well.

Nest was not dead,
but she had thought she was dying
while she was lying there on the rock.
She had prayed to stay alive
till she could see Edward's face once more.

And when she did see it,
white with terror,
bending over her,
she gave a feeble smile,
and let herself faint away once more.

For many months she lay on her bed
unable to move.
delirious – raving
Sometimes she was delirious,
sometimes very depressed.

Through it all,
her mother watched her with tender care.
The neighbours came,
bringing presents and offering help,
but she would let no one else
watch over her child.

For a long time
Edward Williams was always there
asking after Nest,
but by and by he slackened.

At first,
Eleanor thought it was her imagination,
but as time went by,
his coolness was clear to everyone.
The neighbours would have spoke to her
about it,

She didn't want
to talk about it.

but she shrunk from the subject.

But at last she was driven
to her wits' end.
It had been three weeks since Edward had
called,
and Nest was pining away without him.
When Nest was asleep,
Eleanor put on her cloak,
and set off for Edward's farm.

He was looking at some new hay.
When he saw Eleanor,
he blushed, and looked confused.
'It's a fine evening,' he said.
'How is Nest?
Ah, but if you're here
she must be better.
Won't you come in and sit down?'

'No thank you.

balm – a soothing
ointment

The open air is like balm
after being shut up so long.'

'It is a long time,' he replied,
'more than five months.'

'It is a long time, Edward,
since you have been near us
to ask after Nest.
She may be better,
or she may be worse,
for all you know.'

'Well . . . I . . .
you see, the hay has taken a long time,
the weather's been bad,
and . . . and I'm needed here.
Besides, I have seen the doctor,
and he has told me about her.'

Eleanor jumped at this.
'You've seen the doctor.
Oh, man-alive, tell me what he said.
He'll say nothing to me,
but just hems and haws
the more I beg him.
Tell me.'

He tried to avoid the question.

hems and haws –
avoids the question

'It was an unlucky day
that ever she went to the well.'

'Tell me what the doctor said of my child.
Will she live, or will she die?'

'Oh she will live, don't be afraid.
The doctor said she would live ...'

'I am a mother
asking news of my sick child.
Go on! What did he say?
"She'll live ..."'

Eleanor prompts
him.

'Oh, she'll live,
he has no doubts about that.
But ... but ...
I can't tell you.'

'Tell me!
"She'll live, but ..."'

'But ... but ...
she'll be a cripple for life.
There! You have it now.'

'A cripple for life,' she said slowly,
'a cripple for life.'

She sighed heavily.

'And as we're about it,' said Edward hastily,
'I must tell you what is on my mind.
I've a lot of cattle,
and the farm makes heavy work,
as much as a healthy woman can do.
So you see . . .'

He could not finish.
But Eleanor fixed her dark eyes on him.
'Well,' she said at length, 'say on.'

'Well, you must know,
Nest will never be the same again.'

You've not yet
married her.

'And you've not yet sworn before God
to take her for better, or for worse.
And as she is worse,
why, you cast her off,
not being church-tied to her.
Though her body is crippled,
her poor heart is the same – alas –
and full of love for you.'

'But you must see,
Nest will never be fit
to be any man's wife.
I cannot – no one would expect me
to marry a cripple.'

'Very well,' said Eleanor,
and turned to go away.
But then her anger burst from her.
She turned back, and raised her hands to
heaven.

'The widow's child is unfriended.
With my tears I call on God and His angels
to watch over my Nest,
and avenge her cruel wrongs.'

She turned away weeping,
and wringing her hands.
But then she stopped and came back again.

'Forgive me.
Did I curse you?
I beg you to forgive me.
It will kill my Nest
if she knows the truth now –
she is so very weak.
You would not wish to kill her,
I think, Edward?'

Eleanor remembers
that it would kill
Nest if Edward didn't
come to see her.

She looked at him,
as if expecting an answer,
but he did not speak.
She went down on her knees
in front of him.

'You will give me a little more time, Edward,
to get her strong, won't you now?
I ask it on my bended knees!
You will come sometimes to see her,
till she is well enough
to know it's all over,
and her heart's hopes crushed.
Only say you'll come for a month, or so,
as if you still loved her –
the poor cripple –
forlorn – all alone forlorn of the world.'
Her tears fell too fast for her to go on.

'Get up, Mrs Gwynn,' said Edward.
'Don't kneel to me.
I will come and see Nest . . .
I will . . .
now and then.'

II

Nest slowly got better.
Edward did come to see her,
and stayed a quarter of an hour.
He dared not look her in the face.

Nest was indeed a cripple.
One leg was much shorter than the other,
and she limped on a crutch.

Her face was grey
and pale with suffering –
the bright roses were gone,
never to return.
Her large eyes were sunk
deep down in their sockets.

But the light was still in them
when Edward came.

One evening Eleanor steeled herself
and told Nest the truth about Edward.
She made her voice hard and cold
to hide the pain inside her.
She tried to sound reasonable,
but Nest turned away from reason.
She turned away from her mother,
and she turned away from the world.
She bound her sorrow tight up in her breast.

Nest bottled
everything up inside
her.

Night after night,
her mother heard her cries and moans –
more pitiful than her cries of pain
when she fell and hurt herself.
And night after night,
when her mother tried to comfort her,
Nest said there was nothing wrong.

Eleanor prayed every night,
'If only she would open her sore heart to me –
to me, her mother – I would be content.
Once it was enough to have my Nest all my
own.
Then came love,
and I knew it would never be as before.
And then I thought the grief I felt,
when Edward spoke to me,
was as sharp a sorrow as could be.
But this present grief, oh God,
is worst of all.'

The grief is because
Eleanor knows Nest
is in pain,
but won't let her
help her.

When Nest grew as strong
as she was ever likely to be,
all she wanted was hard work.
She would not let her mother spare her.
She wanted hard work to exhaust her
and dull her feelings.
She was almost fierce
when her mother tried to save her
from the jobs she used to do.

exhaust her –
tire her out
completely

Everything was to go on as it had been
before she had known Edward.

And so it did, outwardly.
But they trod carefully,
as if the ground on which they walked
was hollow.

There was no more careless ease –
every word was guarded,
and every action planned.
It was a dreary life for both.

One day news came to Eleanor
that Edward Williams was about to be
married.
She had been expecting this,
and dreading it.
She could not tell Nest.

dreading – fearing

When Nest heard the news,
she came and stood before her mother.
'Mother, why did you not let me die?
Why did you keep me alive for this?'

Eleanor could not speak,
but put her arms out towards her girl.
Nest turned away,
and Eleanor cried out in pain.

Nest turned back.
'I'm sorry, mother.
You did your best.
I don't know how it is
I am so hard and cold.
I wish I had died when I was a girl
and had a feeling heart.'

'Don't speak so, my child.
You have suffered so much,
and your hardness of heart is only for a time.
I understand, I don't mind.
My poor Nest, wait a little,
and your feeling heart will come back to you.'

After this, Eleanor and Nest
were drawn a little more together.

death blow –
a hurt that kills

But all this sorrow was a death blow to
Eleanor.
She did not hide the truth from herself.
She knew she could not comfort
Nest's poor wounded heart,
and she did not wish to live.

'I am weary of earth,' she said.
'But how can I find rest in death
when I leave my child

desolate –
very unhappy

desolate and broken-hearted?'

She sunk very quickly.
She was very calm in death –
no more weeping, no more sorrow.
Her last look was a smile,
her last word a blessing.

laid out –
prepared the body

This was the custom
of the time.

Nest laid out the poor, worn body.
She was tearless.
She laid a plate with salt upon it on the
breast,
and lighted candles for the head and feet.
Then she sat gazing on the dead
with hot, dry eyes.

My body has
changed in shape,
but the biggest
change is inside me.

'She is dead,' said Nest.
'My mother is dead.
No one loves me now.
Love!
What has love done to me?
I was once the beautiful Nest.
I am now a cripple,
a poor, pale-faced cripple,
old before my time.
But that is nothing to the change inside me –
I was gentle once.
If anyone spoke a tender word to me,
my heart went out to them
as natural as a little child
goes to its mother.

I never spoke roughly,
even to dumb animals,
for I had a kind feeling for all.
But now in my thoughts
I am cruel to everyone.'

Her voice sunk to a hoarse whisper.

hardly – cruelly

'I have even spoke hardly of you, mother.
You who was ever patient,
and full of love for me.
You did not know
how I loved you.

solemn – serious

Come back, mother,' she cried wildly,
to the still, solemn corpse,
'come back as a spirit or a ghost –
only come back,
that I may tell you
how I have loved you.'

Nest's outburst ended in tears,
the first she had shed.

When they stopped,
she stood with her head bowed,
quite calm.

III

Many months passed.
Nest carried on living in the cottage,
which was now her own.

There was in the village
a half-witted woman,
a poor, crazy creature,
who was called Mary Williams.
She stayed with John Griffiths,
and was paid for by the church.

The church pays
John to look after her
out of charity.

The villagers called her a savage,
and John used to beat her,
and keep her without food
to try to tame her.
He said there were days
when he used to beat her till she howled,
and still she would not do
as she was told.

Eleanor had spoken kindly to her,
and once or twice given her an oatcake,
or some porridge.

One night she came to Nest's cottage,
all shivering and starved.
She didn't know that Eleanor was dead.

Nest remembered how her mother
used to feed and comfort the poor woman,
and made her some gruel,
and wrapped her by the fire.

The next morning
John came in search of Mary,
and found her with Nest.
wailed so piteously She wailed so piteously
at the sight of him,
that Nest would not let her go.

She said that Mary could stay with her,
and John was pleased to let her go.

And so Mary came to stay with Nest,
and the doors of Nest's heart were opened –
opened wide by the love
she grew to feel for crazy Mary,
so helpless, so friendless,
and needing her so much.

wailed so piteously
– cried and looked
scared

Mary loved her back,
as a dumb animal loves its blind master.
It was happiness enough to be near her.
She was only too glad
to do what she was told by Nest.

But there were times
when Mary was overcome
by the glooms and fancies
of her poor confused brain.

glooms and fancies
– wild, depressing
thoughts

Then she would pace
forwards and backwards in some wild mood,
making sounds that were scarcely human.

And Nest, cripple that she was,
would walk with her,
speaking low soothing words,
until the pace was eased.
Then Nest would put her arms around her,
and by this tender caress
soothe her into tears –
tears which gave relief to the hot brain.

And so the years passed,
and Nest kept Mary with her all the time.

Because of her accident,
Nest grew old before her time.
She was as old at fifty
as many are at seventy.

Memories came back to her.
She dreamt of her girlhood, and youth.
In sleep she was once more
the beautiful Nest Gwynn,
the light-hearted girl
beloved of her mother.

fatal –
causing death

With these memories came a desire
to see the beautiful fatal well again.
She had never been back there,
since the day she had lost love, and hope,
and her bright glad youth.

She longed to look upon its waters once
again.

The desire grew on her.
She told it to poor crazy Mary.

'Mary,' she said.
I want to go to the Rock Well.
If you will help me,
I can manage it.
We will go tomorrow
before anyone else is up.'

Mary answered, 'Up, up!
To the Rock Well.
Mary will go.
Mary will go.'

Nest had the happiest dream that night.
Her mother seemed to be standing by her,
and stretching out her arms to her
with a calm glad look of welcome.

When she awoke,
the birds were singing in the woods close by.

Nest got up and called Mary.
The two set out through the quiet lane.
They went along slowly and silently.

With many stops they made their way
carefully over the sloping stones
until they came to the well.

The clear water sparkled in the early
sunlight,
the ferns hung wet and dripping
where the water overflowed,
and the running stream sang
low and soft and sweet.

All was the same.

It might have been yesterday
that Edward Williams had overtaken her,
and told her his love.

She thought of his words,
and his handsome looks,
and then she remembered the fatal wintry
morning
when joy and youth had fled.

And as she remembered the pain
she felt then,
a new pain came over her,
a real pain, not an echo of the past.

She leant her back against a rock,
without a moan or sigh, and died!

She was so calm and peaceful that Mary,
who had been dipping her fingers in the well
and letting the water run over them,
thought she was asleep,
and carried on playing quietly.

At last she turned and said,
'Mary is tired.
Mary wants to go home.'

Nest did not speak.
Mary repeated her words.
She stood and looked
till she grew frightened.

'Nest, wake!
Nest, wake!'
she said, wildly shaking the form.
But Nest did not wake.

And the first person
who came to the well that morning,
found crazy Mary sitting, awe-struck,
by the poor dead Nest.
They had to get the poor creature
away by force,
before they could remove the body.

They treat her kindly these days,
and usually she is very good.
Sometimes the old wildness comes over her,
and she is out of control.
Then someone will say 'Nest' to her,
and she will stop still,
and make a great effort
to calm herself.
Then she will say.
'Mary has tried to be good.
Can Mary go to Nest now?'

awe-struck –
dumb with fear